The Seven Doors

written by Alanna Zabel

Illustrated by Mary-Margaret Mitchell

Dedicated to:
Sri Aurobindo, Ramana Maharishi,
Paramahansa Yogananda, Vijay
and Deepak Chopra

AZIAM
BOOKS

Published by AZIAM Press
© 2004 Alanna Zabel
ALL rights reserved
www.aziam.com

Ruby was a fun girl
She was always the life of a party
But when it came to school or homework
She was disinterested and tardy

Her soccer coach knew
that she wouldn't practice drills
But when it came to game time
she was nothing shy of thrills

"Ruby has so much potential," her coaches and teachers said
Her parents agreed and replied, "But she is too wild to be led"

People doted on Ruby, praising her many talents and strengths
But she didn't like the attention, that she didn't ask for or create

Since Ruby's talents came so naturally
she didn't know that she was great
you earn the precious gift of self-worth
when you work to manifest your fate

She traveled around the world, without a goal or destination
Everywhere that Ruby went became a magical occasion

Strolling between two towns
Ruby found herself inside a forest
As she sat on a rock to rest
She heard a distant chorus

"Where is that singing coming from?" Ruby asked
Turning her ear towards the sound
A light appeared and she heard these words
"Follow me and you will be found"

The Light moveD to the Right
ILLuminating a Path
"Do not be afRaiD," it saiD
AnD the Light gRew wiDe anD vast

Ruby stePPeD onto the Path
AsKing, "wheRe Does this Path LeaD?"
"TRust me anD stay aLeRt," it saiD
"AnD youR DhaRma you wiLL see"

"what is my DhaRma?" asKeD Ruby
The Light fLicKeReD anD KinDLy LaugheD
"onLy you can DiscoveR youR PuRPose," it saiD
"It is youR onLy tasK"

"I'm getting scared," Ruby said
"With all this talk of the dark"
"Do not be afraid," Ahanna replied
"The dark is more afraid of your spark"

"To live your fullest and best,
keep your heart beaming bright
Light is Truth, Love and Peace
with nothing hidden in the night"

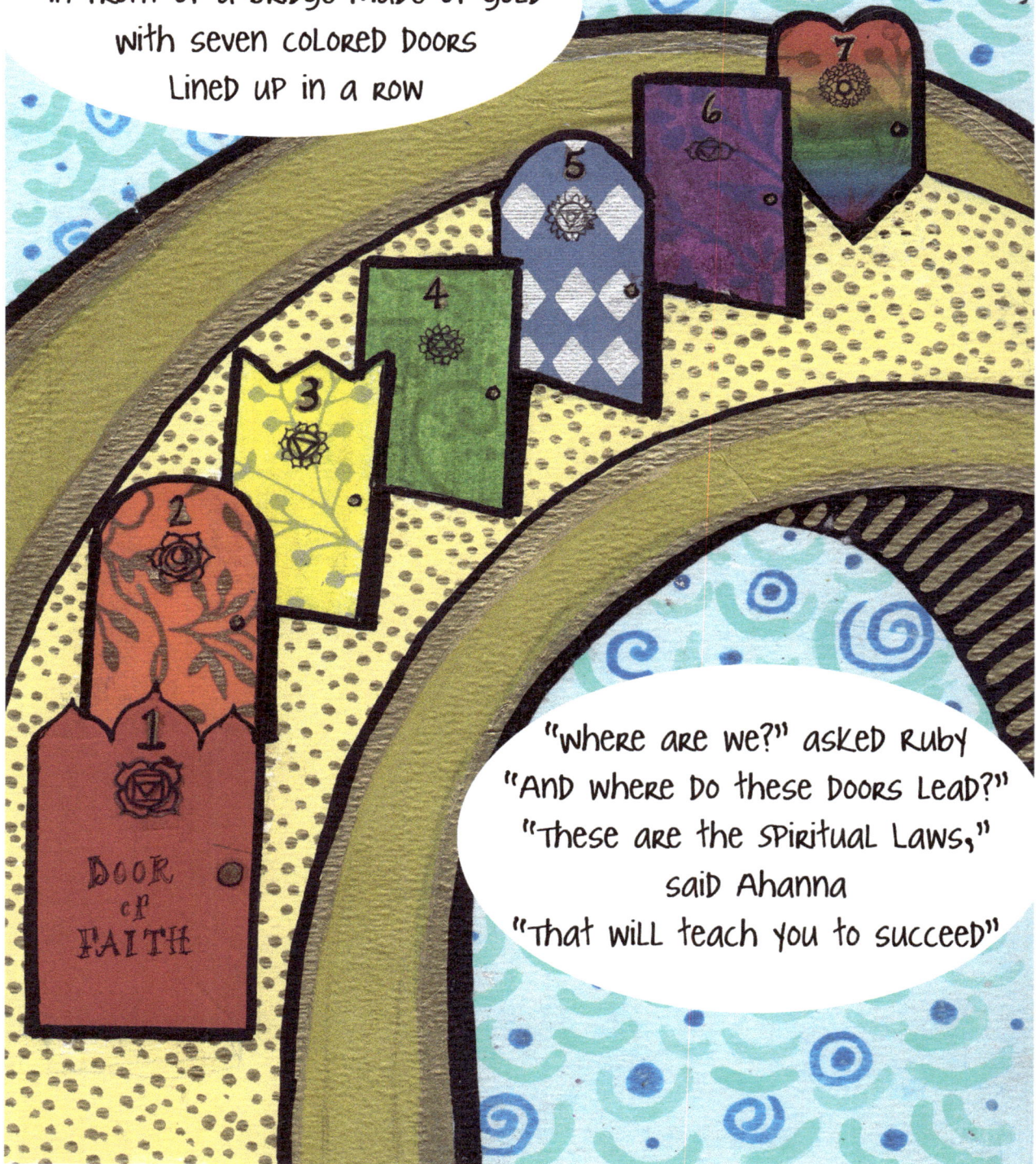

"Pass through the Seven Doors to understand your Purpose"
"When you find your best talent, it will be your greatest service"

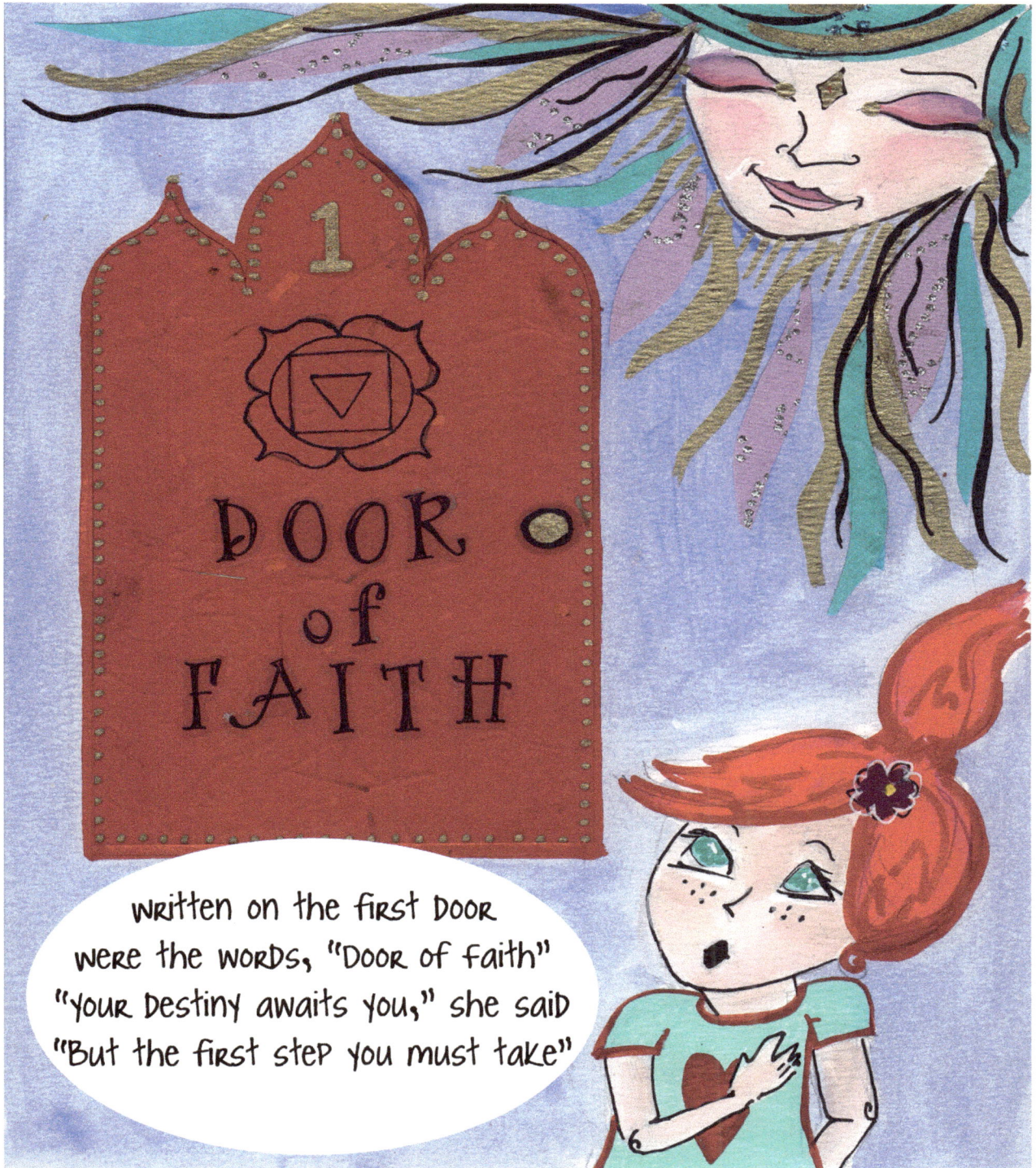

1

DOOR
of
FAITH

Written on the first Door
were the words, "Door of Faith"
"Your destiny awaits you," she said
"But the first step you must take"

LAW #1: PURE POTENTIALITY

Her Desire to share her Joy
Allowed the second Door to appear
But to Leave this magical bliss
Is exactly what she feared
2
"Move through the second Door"
Ruby heard Ahanna say
"You will return to pure potential
Again some other Day"

She gazed beyond the second door
until an image took a shape
She saw sad and lonely people
Not knowing that happiness is their true state

watching the image of lonely people
made Ruby long to make them laugh
Her desire to create a change
sent her through the second door fast

Ruby tried to understand
why the people were lonely and sad
They all had family, friends and abundance
But they didn't know the value of what they had

Silently Ruby asked Ahanna
"How can I help these people live?"
She felt Ahanna reply,
"The second law is to give"

Soon everyone in the park
Started to smile too
But the fact that Ruby was the light
No one but Nana knew

Ruby's presence taught the people
The second Law of Giving
The circulation of your energy
Is the formula for healthy living

Whatever one gives
One will receive
Being afraid to share
May result in greed

The positive energy grew
Making the cloud layer melt
The third door appeared in the sky
"It's time to move on," Ruby felt

As Ruby Jumped towards the Door
She was Pulled through the open gate
She closed her eyes and surrendered
so that she wouldn't hesitate

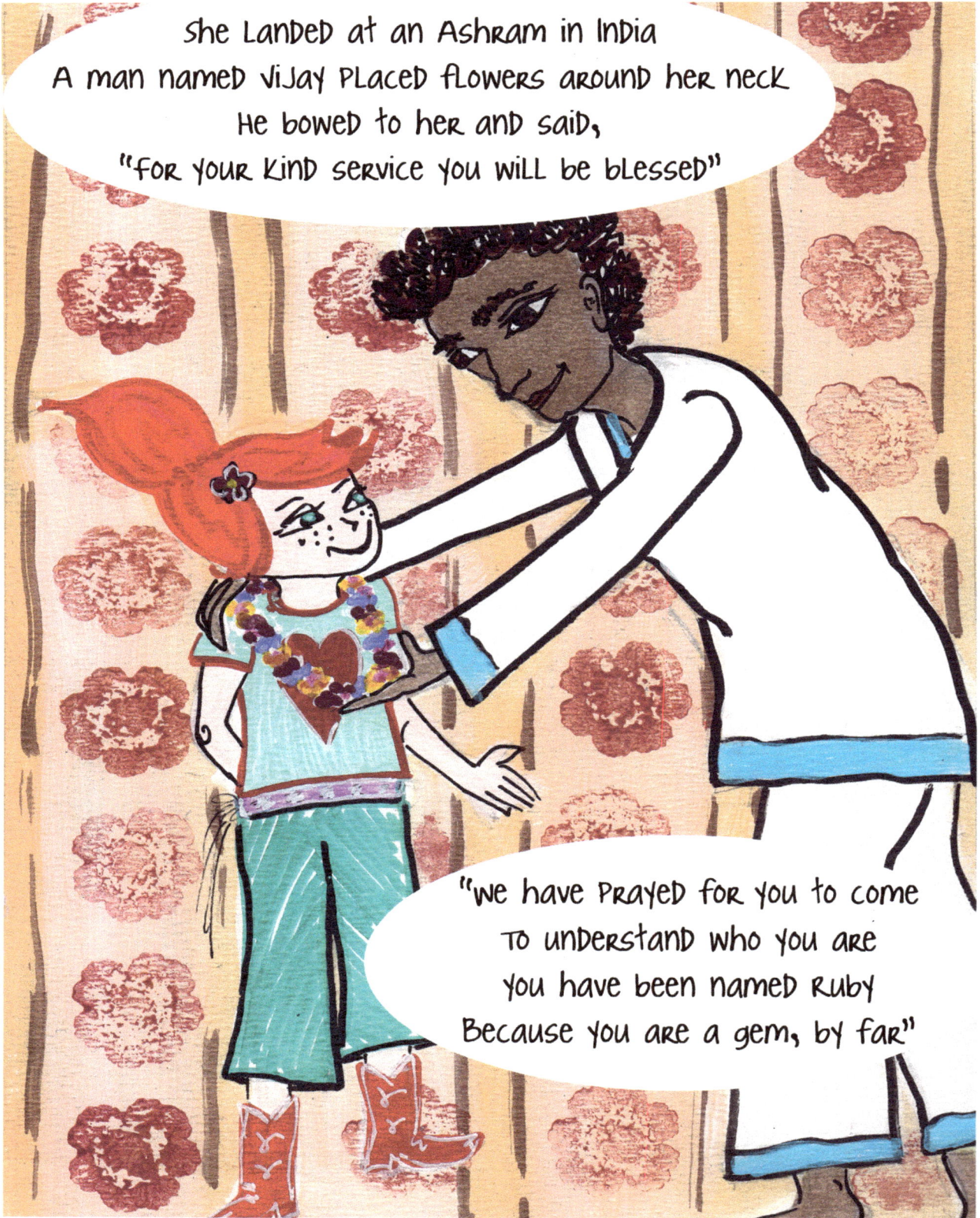

Ruby saw a clock on the wall set to the day and time of her birth
There was thunder and lightning, and shaking of the earth

Vijay handed Ruby a card which read,
"Your birthday is the most receptive time of your year.
Accept my silent gift of love
There is no coincidence you are here"

"You have given so freely to others," Vijay said
"What one gives, one receives
This is the universal law of karma
"Whether or not one believes"

"You have helped others to understand who they are
without asking for anything back
You are here to receive self-realization
And to know that there is nothing that you lack"

when Ruby opened her eyes again
she was standing on the gold bridge once more
three doors surrounded her in a circle
Each one was marked "Number four"

"which one do I enter?" Ruby asked
"They all look alike"
she heard Ahanna's voice
"the one that opens with ease is right"

when Ruby Realized what her actions were creating
she sat Down in front of the next Door
understanding that it DiDn't heLP
To Put out unnecessary effort anymore

she sat for some time
staring at the obstacLe on her Path
she was no Longer frustrateD
AnD from her efforts she DetacheD

she sigheD and closeD her eyes
Letting go of effort aLL at once
she feLt a breeze on her face
AnD the warmth of the sun

She remembered the blissful feelings
That she had felt in Pure Potentiality
She visualized the fourth door open
And it instantly became reality

When Ruby stopped taking action
The fourth door opened easily
This is the Law of Least Effort
Natural synchronicity

Law #6:
LEAST EFFORT

The fifth Law is Intention and Desire
Ruby stopped using force to open the Door
Her mental intention and Desire to open it
Allowed the Possibility to be born

When you Plant a seed of intention
Into the fertile ground of Potential
Your Dreams will take root
Becoming Physical from mental

Law #5:
INTENTION & DESIRE

Ahanna's Light appeared
She said, "You have Learned three Laws at once
The sixth Law of Detachment
Allows for your Desires to be Done"

"once your seed has taken root
You have to Let it go
Nurture your intention with Love
And simply watch it grow"

Law #6:
DETACHMENT

Ruby opened her eyes
She looked at the doors
The numbers had changed to five and six
on the two doors that once read four

For the first time during this challenge
of learning the last three laws
Ruby hadn't thought about the lonely people
or pondered how to find a cause

There was a newfound sense of ease
That Ruby now expressed
She visualized a world of peace
without uncertainty or stress

The three Doors merged together
To form the seventh Door
It was a heart-shaped rainbow
with a Large ruby at its core

"This is the seventh Law of Dharma," Ahanna said
"The union of your self with your spirit
you need not force your Destiny
Nor will you ever fear it"

Law 7   Dharma

As this door opened, Ruby saw a Light similar to Pure Potentiality
There was a warmth Ruby felt - a sense of familiarity

She heard Ahanna's voice, "Ruby you have merged completely with me"
"We will walk in Truth and Light, together, until Eternity"

"You will always be on the right path
you will never hesitate or fear
your life will reveal itself
every step will be clear"
"You have reached the state of union
of your soul and human form
Ask yourself how you can serve
This is the reason you were born"

Ruby walked through the Rainbow Door
Again she heard a Distant chorus
She smiled and Laughed out Loud
As she found herself back in the forest

She continued with her traveling
Much Like she had done before
But now she understood her purpose
And she wasn't searching anymore

Ruby found her mission
without giving it a second thought
How to Live the Laws of Spirituality
Is exactly what she taught

She realized that her talents
were giving Love and Laughter
To create peace and harmony
forever, ever after

Ruby became a teacher of yoga
Teaching the Laws of Giving and karma
using the Laws of Least Effort, Intention and Detachment
To unfold one's true Dharma

we already have all the answers
Hidden within our souls
The moment that we unite with our spirit
Is when we reach our final goal

I hope that these laws assist you
In uniting your body to your soul

And that you live a miraculous life of Grace

Everywhere that you go...

Om Shanti
ૐ

Namasté,

Alanna

WHO AM I?

1) what makes me the most happy? _____

_____

_____

2) what are my favorite gifts to give? _____

_____

_____

3) what are my favorite activities? _____

_____

_____

4) who Do I Like to heLP? _____

_____

_____

5) what change would I Like to see in the world? _____

_____

_____

6) In all of history, who Do I Look up to as a role model? _

_____

_____

7) How can I help the world to be a better place? _____

_____

_____

Glossary

Ahimsa: No action creates any harm to any creature. Choose actions that bring joy and happiness to yourself and others.

Ananda: Bliss and joy!

Asana: The practice of hatha yoga as a means to align and purify the body.

Detachment: The Sixth Law. Letting go of force, expectation and activity to allow Nature to work. If something if meant to happen, it will.

Dharana: Minimizing distractions and increasing focus. Ex: stare at the tip of your nose for 15 minutes.

Dharma: The Seventh Law. Your greatest talent and your destined purpose for being.

Dhyana: Meditation. The practice of still awareness

Giving: The second Law. Offering a physical or energetic gift to someone without expecting anything in return.

Intention: The fifth Law. Having a mental desire that is harmonious with universal Dharma.

karma: The third Law of cause and effect. What you give, you will receive. Do unto others as you'd have done to you.

Least Effort: The fourth Law. Make choices using the Law of Least resistance.

Namaste': Translated "The Light within me recognizes the Light within you."

Niyama: Living a Life of Purity and cleanliness.

om: The Purest sound essence of "I AM".

Pure Potentiality: The First Law. The empty, void-of-thought space where creation begins.

Pranayama: Moving energy throughout your body with various breathing exercises.

Pratyahara: Withdrawing from your senses and Personal Desires to witness the Power of Nature and Self.

Samadhi: Blissful oneness.

Shanti: Peace

Yama: Always be kind and tell the truth.

Yoga: union

CPSIA information can be obtained
at www.ICGtesting.com
Printed in the USA
LVHW072151270219
609001LV00002B/4/P